How To Get To The Other Side

ZACHARY BREWSTER, SR.

Dedication

This book is dedicated to my Hero,
Suzanne Virginia Pinson Brewster.
Thank you for being a mother who
always made me believe that I could
reach my dreams!

CONTENTS

1

BEGINNING THE JOURNEY

"WARREN IVERSON NICHOLS." As I crossed the stage hearing the unauthorized cheers, seeing cameras flash and preparing for a firm handshake, it felt like I was standing on top of the world. Sam Love stepped out of line to give me a big bear hug as I exited the stage and the two of us prepared for what was sure to be an epic summer. It was the summer before we left home to continue the party on the coast at The College of Charleston. I would write more about that summer, however, due to our "*to-the-grave*" agreement and the fact that much of it is a blur, I'll spare you the details. I do remember the fact that it passed a lot faster than we expected and we were saying goodbye to our parents who gave too many warnings and too little spending money. Now it was time to make connections and enjoy our first night of freedom prior to the required freshman seminar at 8 a.m. the following day.

It was a great night and an early morning as we sprinted into the auditorium right past the coffee and continental breakfast straight to the vending machine for a Coke and then to find a seat in the balcony. For most of the seminar we heard the typical freshman orientation speeches mixed with faculty, alumni and upper classmen. Right before we decided that there was no way we'd make it through the last four speakers, one of the professors who was ending his speech asked an interesting question, "How will you get to the other side?"

After Professor Humbert phrased this question I remember thinking to myself, "The other side of what?" He continued his 12-minute monologue with Socratic statements that left me searching for answers that I realized didn't exist within me at the time. When he finished, the other three speakers spoke for 15 minutes each, and though I stayed in my seat, I never heard a word they said. We were dismissed to meet and greet each other as well as the presenters, but to my disappointment, I was unable to find Professor Humbert. We left that day with two days before classes officially began. After three dorm room parties, six bars, four clubs and a trip to the beach, I was ready to begin my college career. The first day was spent locating buildings, reviewing jaw dropping syllabi and attempting not to run into the people in front of me as I experienced the head turning joys of attending a school with a 13:1 female to male ratio. 2:40 p.m. arrived and I made my way back toward my dorm, frustrated that no one told me that 8 a.m. courses are not required.

At the cross walk I saw him coming in a full suit, bow-tie, briefcase and an unlit pipe. I stood still and waited until he crossed over to my side and as he came near I said, "Are you Professor Humbert?" "Last I checked." he replied "and you are?" "Warren Nichols", I said as I extended my hand. He gave me what felt like the firmest handshake I'd ever received and then continued to walk past me.

Should I follow him, I asked myself. *I wonder where he's headed.* As I pondered these questions in my mind, he faded further away. After standing there wishing I had just asked him to clarify what had now become an annoying question, Sam walked up. We walked towards the library to attempt to make sense of a very tumultuous day but the interaction that I had with Professor Humbert still lingered in my mind.

The next morning arrived and no matter how many times I hit snooze, my 8 a.m. course was still at the same time. I finally rolled out of bed and followed seemingly the same routine as the day before. Crosswalks, search buildings for parties, stares, smiles and finally locating my class. At 8:25 a.m. I arrived at my Public Speaking 101 course. There was only one door so unfortunately I had to enter the front of the room, after the door had already been closed. "MR. NICHOLS", I heard in a very commanding voice. I turned around to my surprise to see a bow-tie and an unlit pipe. "Good morning", I said. Professor Humbert went on to ask me if I made a habit of showing up at destinations after the pre-determined time of arrival. Sam was already seated and enjoying my persecution with the rest of the class. After several minutes, Professor Humbert finally showed me a little mercy and continued on with the course. He handed me a syllabus that was very different than the four I received the day before. Public Speaking 101 was at the top, however, there were very few instructions following the heading. No due dates, grading scale, term paper requirements or dates of exams; it was simply a one-page document that listed course dates, times, his contact information and an image with a question:

How Will You Get To The Other Side?

He informed us that we only had one speech to prepare and we would have the entire semester to develop it. This speech would not be uniquely designed relating to a topic of our choice but would very simply answer the previously stated question, *'How Will You Get To The Other Side?'* He said that with of all the courses that we would take, lectures we would attend, interesting people we would meet and questions that we would encounter, answering this question would put all of those interactions into perspective. When he asked for questions, I scanned the room and no one budged. I slowly began to lift my hand and it felt as if the eyes of those who sat on either side of me would maul me beyond recognition. Everyone knows that the first day of class is short and sweet if you survive the review of the syllabus and never ask a single question. Needless to say, I folded under the pressure of my peers and Professor Humbert said, "Once again, anxiety has annihilated analysis." Hearing no response to his profound and deafening statement, he dismissed the class.

After class I hung around to talk to Professor Humbert. He told me that I was welcome to chat but that we had to walk and talk. I waited until he packed his briefcase and we headed out the door to stroll across campus. I told him that his question really stuck out in my mind during the freshman seminar and how excited I was to be his class to get some closure. I started rambling in overload! I let him know that I wasn't really clear on what the other side was or how to focus on getting there and how unsure I was about even going.

"Why didn't you pose this inquiry in the presence of your peers?", he asked. I dropped my head and didn't respond. He smiled and instead of answering my question, he confused me even more. He said, "The other side can only be determined based on your destination. How you get there is derived from your present location. Achieving the journey is a matter of motivation." When he finished I just stood there silently. By that time we had arrived at a bench and he sat down, reached in his bag and pulled out his pipe. After lighting it, he crossed his legs and looked up towards me as I stood waiting for him to continue. He stated, "Nichols, it appears that you are seeking something that you intend to find. Meet me on the corner of Calhoun and East Bay on Saturday morning at 7 a.m. if you're interested in continuing the journey."

Points to Ponder

- We are all on a journey whether we're certain of where we're headed or not.
- Questions that we cannot answer often serve as defining moments.
- You must be willing to sacrifice to obtain what you desire.

"The other side can only be determined based on your destination. How you get there is derived from your present location; achieving the journey is a matter of motivation."

2
A FIRM FOUNDATION

IT'S SATURDAY MORNING at 6:47 a.m. and I'm standing on the corner of Calhoun and East Bay Street contemplating what would take place today. I decided to wear slacks and the blazer that my Dad bought me for graduation that I would *"need-for-the-real-world"* and this was that type of moment.

"Mr. Nichols." I turned around and saw Professor Humbert quickly approaching. "A little over-dressed for the journey are we?" To my surprise there was no suit, bow-tie, pipe or brief case. Instead, he wore a pair of running shoes, a hooded sweatshirt that read "a mind is a terrible thing to waste " and a pair of sweat pants. I shook my head and smiled at his unpredictable nature. "I'll be right back," he said. Five minutes later he pulled up in a burgundy 1978 Dodge Minivan. I guess the look on my face said it all when I got in because he said, "They don't make cars like they used to, even after all these years, this car runs like the day I first bought it!" We turned left onto East Bay Street as the sun was beginning to rise. "Where are you from Sir?", he inquired. I told him that I was from Greenville, South Carolina. "Ahhhh what a beautiful place," he said. "what brings you here to Charleston?" Due to the depth of his questions, I tried to be more eloquent than just saying 'school'. "I chose Charleston because I realize that it is a place that offers opportunities to learn both educationally and historically!" He looked over at me, smiled and said, "So which part of the historical nature of Charleston interests you the most?" I fumbled and mumbled a bit and frowned like I was in deep thought. Finally he said "There have been many young men who have confused history and education for beaches and other beauties." I lowered my head so he wouldn't see me blush and turn red, however, I'm sure he caught a glimpse. We arrived in a parking lot right before the exit to enter onto the Cooper River Bridge. He got out of the car and I followed. He walked to the end of the lot to a fence that faced the bridge. As we stood there he stared in silence for what seemed like forever, and though I wanted to ask what we were looking for, I never said a word. He turned to me and said, "Nichols, this is the product of progress."

"Progress?" I asked.

"Yes PROGRESS!", he said in a resounding voice.
He then began an address that was worthy to be played on Broadway, which made me feel a little less awkward about being in a blazer:

"The definition of *progress* is to move toward a goal or a higher stage. There was a time when the Cooper River represented a separation between where we stand and what we now know as Mount Pleasant. In 1928, John P. Grace answered a question that we all must address in our lives; *HOW WILL I GET TO THE OTHER SIDE?* He wasn't the only one who had this wish, hope or desire yet he was the only one who devoted the necessary attention to take things from wishing, hoping and desiring to making it a way of life. There were 2.7 miles between him and his destiny, which is a little less than what we would now call a 5k. He made a decision that though it seemed improbable, it was not impossible to accomplish. The question that I posed to you and your peers is not a trick question, it's a question that's vital to your very existence. Grace knew what the other side was, he could stand here just like us and see it. In order for you to be capable of answering the question, there are four questions that you must encounter:

1. What is the starting point of your *Migration*?
2. What is your final *Objective*?
3. In order to get from one place to another, what will be your *Vehicle*?
4. Prior to taking the first step, have you examined what you'll *Endure*?

Once you wrestle with these questions and victoriously arrive at the answers, you will then be ready to *M.O.V.E.* College for many students represents an expeditious experience to locate the person that they've been connected to and unsuccessfully identified for 18 years. For those few who have discovered themselves, their maneuvers are filled with productive processes to ensure that their goals are accomplished. For those who mirror the majority, they are often left preoccupied with the indecisiveness of where they are headed."

After he finished his oration, he turned around and faced me instead of the bridge. "Nichols, I see a lot of potential inside of you; let me know when you're ready to M.O.V.E." Once he said that, he turned and walked back toward the van. I followed him slowly as I digested his words and wondered how I would respond. What was amazing was that although I hadn't taken a single note, I remembered every word he said to me. There was complete silence on the trip back other than Professor Humbert asking which dorm I lived in. Once we arrived at the corner of Wentworth and Coming Street, I exited the van and thanked him for taking time with me. He smiled and said, "I'm always available if you want or need to talk." When he pulled off, I ran straight to my room. I grabbed a notepad and wrote the four questions that he said I must encounter and I made a commitment to answer them that day.

Unfortunately a week later I still hadn't answered the first one. I realized that I was a part of the majority of students that Professor Humbert spoke about. Those who arrive on campus with no idea of who they are, where they're going and what they'd like to do with their lives. Only a couple of weeks earlier I thought I knew. I came to CofC because my parents determined that my second choice was more economical than my first in Chapel Hill. My plan was to major in business so that it would be the perfect complement to Sam's degree in Hospitality and Tourism. Together, we were going to open the best nightlife attractions that Charleston had ever seen. Once I attempted to actually answer the questions, things didn't seem so clear anymore.

In October, most of us decided that we weren't going home for fall break; there was a high chance that we were on the brink of the last opportunity to hang out at the beach while it was still warm. One night on the way back from the Isle of Palms, I felt like someone shined a flood light in my face. We were on the Cooper River Bridge and I asked them to stop the car. After being called crazy among a lot of other names, I settled for lowering my window and gazing from one bridge to the other. When we got back downtown, I skipped the routine trip to Sharky's Pizza and went back to my room. I located the spiral notebook where I had written Professor Humbert's questions. I couldn't wait, so I called him right then and to my surprise he was sitting in his office at 10:16 p.m. on a Friday night. Although I was shocked to hear his voice, I think he was just as shocked to hear mine. "Mr. Nichols," he said "is everything ok Sir?"

"Not only is everything ok, it's great!!!", I said. "I think I'm ready to M.O.V.E now!"

I asked if he had some time after fall break for me to stop by his office and share my thoughts. He said, "Mr. Nichols, is there a reason that you would hold your motivation captive for several days? If not, I'll wait here in my office until you get here tonight." When I hung up the phone I couldn't believe that I was headed to meet with a Professor on a Friday night. I decided not to tell anyone where I was going for fear they would have me tested for illegal substances.

When I arrived at his office, I could smell the pipe from the porch. I walked in and went upstairs to find him sitting on the ledge of the window looking out onto the campus. He stood up to extend his hand and I braced myself for the vice grip. Once he returned to his desk I decided to stand while I spoke and while I was nowhere near being ready for Broadway, I think the Dock Street Theatre would have appreciated what I had to say.

That night I realized that the starting point of my migration was not merely a question regarding what school I chose or what I would declare as a major, my migration began with my upbringing and included all of the things that shaped me to be the person that I am today. Gaining an understanding of what influences contributed to my make-up helped me determine my true identity. Understanding my temperament was even more important than trying to comprehend exactly what I wanted to do in life because knowing myself would help me decide on what my future should be.

My final objective didn't have to be as detailed as I once thought. It wasn't imperative for me to know exactly what company I wanted to work for and how soon I wanted to be promoted. I didn't have to know who I would marry and whether we wanted two or three kids and a dog. It wasn't essential that I know the car I would drive, the house that I would buy or even the state or city that I would live in.

The truth is that even though John P. Grace knew that he wanted to get from one side of the shore to the other, he had no way of grasping all of the possibilities that were present in Mount Pleasant. He couldn't have envisioned the businesses, the homes, the golf courses or all the wonderful things that Mount Pleasant or even Charleston in comparison to the late 1920's would eventually have to offer. All he knew was that his final objective was to get there or else him, or nobody else, would have the chance to explore what could transpire. I processed the fact that my objective is only required to be sound enough to encompass the general destination of my journey, not all of the unfeasible details.

The vehicle for my journey is the same one Grace used; a bridge. A bridge is a structure that provides a connection between two elements. Just like Grace, I needed to start at the very beginning. From this point on, each season of my life would contribute to the construction of my bridge.

I've accepted the fact that life will always present its' share of obstacles. The challenge that we often face is that we get so distracted by the presence of the obstruction, we lack the endurance to overcome the problem. After examining the probability of life's many difficulties, I've decided that I will endure whatever I must to achieve my goals.

When I was finished, Professor Humbert stood up and gave me a long stare. He finally broke the silence and said "Well said Mr. Nichols, well said." I extended my hand to him and he came around his desk and hugged me instead. His embrace was an added bonus to celebrate my epiphany. When I left his office that night, I started writing my speech for Public Speaking 101 answering the question *"How will you get to the other side?"*

I was ready to finish classes and go home for the holidays but when I arrived in class the following day after completing my speech, it was different than all of the other days. Everyone appeared to be very concerned about the speech and what questions Professor Humbert would ask but I was very confident that he would appreciate the level of focus and determination I placed on determining the answer to the question. When I stood up in front of the room, I suddenly recognized the impact that Professor Humbert had made in my life. At that moment I viewed my presentation as much more than just a required speech but as an opportunity to change lives the way mine had been. I opened my speech by telling the class about John P. Grace and his dream of getting to the other side. I then informed them that

I had decided to build a bridge just like he did and that the next four years represented the first step.

In order to build a bridge you must first begin with a firm foundation. The foundation, or *"footing"* as it's sometimes referred to, rests directly on the soil and is typically below grade and therefore not visible. Although this portion of the bridge is often not apparent, it is crucial to the rest of the structure. I enlightened them to the fact that during college years, many students use it as a time to succumb to the distractions and assign the bare minimum level of attention to developing the essential skills to be successful in their careers. Their philosophy is that a college degree alone is enough of a foundation to build from. On the contrary, although a college degree is often foundational, there are so many other elements needed to ensure that it is firm enough to withstand all of the other materials that must rest upon it to complete the bridge. As a result, research shows that 63% of college students that obtain an internship while in school are extended a job offer when they graduate. In comparison, only 40% of students who do not intern are offered a job. This same survey showed that 44% of employers prefer candidates with an internship or work during college on their resume vs. only 13% factoring in a college major in their decision-making and less than 10% focusing on GPA. This is proof that in order to build a firm foundation, it's going to require you to do more than surface level work. When the construction companies establish the foundation, they must ensure that they have reached a solid portion of the soil that will be able to support the weight of the structure. You must use the time that you have as a student to assure you've reached solid ground.

Points to Ponder

- **M.O.V.E**
  1. What is the starting point of your *Migration*?
  2. What is your final *Objective*?
  3. In order to get from one place to another, what will be your *Vehicle*?
  4. Prior to taking the first step, have you examined what you'll *Endure*?
- Statistics prove that young adults who obtain experience in college are more valued by employees vs. students who simply achieve a degree.

"In order to build a bridge you must first begin with a firm foundation. The foundation or "footing" as it's sometimes referred to rests directly on the soil; it's typically below grade and therefore not visible. Although this portion of the bridge is often not apparent, it is crucial to the rest of the structure."

3
THE TOWERS

"WARREN IVERSON NICHOLS." Who knew that four years would go so quickly. As I crossed the stage in the Kress Arena during the December graduation, I felt like I was really ready to enter the real world. Although I hadn't received a job offer yet, I had completed two internships, worked for two different companies over the summers and served in several leadership groups on campus. My resume was drawing attention from area employers and I was confident that it would only be a matter of time. After a family dinner filled with the emotion of congratulatory speeches and gifts, I headed home again for the holidays. My mom comforted me with the understanding that most companies slow their recruiting efforts in the fourth quarter and that I'd probably hear something right after the New Year. I took joy in her perspective and had a very enjoyable Christmas. On January 4th, I made it back to Charleston and prepared for work the next day. I was grateful that the Front

Desk Manager at the hotel was kind enough to give me the flexibility to take three weeks off. Each day at work I constantly checked my email during down time and called home to check my voicemail to ensure that I hadn't missed any calls. I was thankful that I actually had a job that would pay the bills and keep my account out of the negative but this wasn't what I expected when I received my Bachelor's Degree in Business Administration with a minor in Corporate Communications. I mean, most of my co-workers were either still in college or had no formal education at all. Had I fallen into the 37% of College Students that hadn't received an offer even though they had completed the internships and possessed work experience during college? By April, I had drastically reduced my '10-resume-a-day' strategy and was only searching for jobs once every couple of weeks. I won the Front Desk drawing to see who would be off during the Cooper River Bridge Run that year and let Sam twist my arm to run it for the first time. I had no interest in piling up with a bunch of people on a bridge and running across just for the t-shirt.

That morning we took the bus over to Mount Pleasant and waited for them to finish the opening ceremony and release the masses. There were thousands of people there but there was one person that I could pick out of a crowd anywhere; Professor Humbert. I walked over to say hello and he was just as excited to see me. After we embraced like long lost friends, I asked how his sabbatical in Kenya had gone. He said that it was a *"mountain top"* experience and that I must visit at some point in my life. As usual, he was dressed a little differently than everyone else sporting a long sleeved sweat shirt that read "reading is fundamental" with a pair of shorts, high topped tennis shoes and a stop watch around his neck. I often wanted to inquire about his attire but resisted the temptation due to the uncertainty of his response. I did ask him about the stop watch though and he said, "Mr. Nichols, I have discovered that I am the only one who is truly capable of evaluating my pace in life." Almost as soon as he said this, the gun went off and the run began. I decided to stay back and walk with him instead of running. During our walk, he would often glance at his stop watch for a moment and then continue. Finally, I asked him if it would bother him if we talked along the way. "Not at all," he said, "just understand that my responses will not be as long-winded due to the portion of wind that I must reserve to complete the journey."

"No problem, Sir," I said as I chuckled to myself. I asked him what he meant when he said that he was the only person that could evaluate his pace. I asked because the numbers that each participant receives for the Bridge Run had a magnetic indicator that allowed for the officials to track each person's time. As a result, they're able to not only determine the winner, but also each person's official time. He just looked at me and smiled. After we made it up the ramp and began crossing the bridge, he finally responded to my question. "Mr. Nichols, the officials of the run report the time to each person at the finish line and while that's significant in determining how long it took for you to get from point A to point B, it lacks an extremely important element. The time it takes to get to the end doesn't inform me of where I am in relation to my expected pace during the incremental portions of my journey. I carry a stop watch because I not only want to know how long it takes me to get from the beginning to the end but where I am at each phase. Based on my personal knowledge of how I prepared for the journey and what I want to accomplish, I am able to determine if my pace meets my standards. In life we often are met with unsettling emotions due to the pace of other people. When we see others going faster than us, we fear that we'll be left behind. When we see others moving slower than us, we often move to rush with haste just to experience the pride of saying we were ahead of them. That's why I'm unmoved by the rate in which all of these other participants travel. Their speed does not indicate whether I'm behind or ahead, only my timer."

When he finished his explanation, my mind drifted back to the day he drove me over to see the bridge and once again he had given me so much to consider. Once we made it to the finish line we walked to the market to talk more. I told him that I had become discouraged with my job search and that his insight regarding the stopwatch really gave me some food for thought. He reminded me that I had established a firm foundation and that even the job that I had at the hotel was the beginning of my *Tower.*

Seeing the confusion on my face, he explained: "The tower of a bridge is the tall pier or frame that supports the cable of a suspension bridge. The tower is built upon the foundation and is constructed at an immense altitude for all to see. This tower is just like the career aspirations of those who enter into the workforce. Everyone desires to be on the fast-track in a field that offers them the opportunity for elevation. It is a reasonable expectation to want all of those things out of an occupation but just know that the tower is built high in order to assist in supporting other materials, therefore, we cannot become fixated on the highest point of the tower because the tower is not the portion of the bridge on which you stand. Nonetheless, you must ensure that your tower ranges high enough. So, what you must determine when you're considering career choices is, does it meet the necessary specifications of my *T.O.W.E.R.?*"

He wrote those letters just like that on a napkin and pushed it over to me. I borrowed a pen from the waitress and asked her for extra napkins as I prepared to take notes while Professor Humbert continued:

1. Is pursuing this job opening a decision that is *Tactical*?
2. Does this role provide me with *Options*?
3. Have I determined for myself what I am *Worth*?
4. Is this a transitionary opportunity or a place where I can be *Embedded*?
5. Does this opportunity add value to my projected *Results*?

These questions totally reshaped my perspective as it related to the status of my career. I returned to work that Monday afternoon with a new attitude. Over the weekend I discovered that my job as a Front Desk Representative at the hotel was a transitionary opportunity as it related to my *T.O.W.E.R.* As a result, there were things that I could learn while I continued to evaluate the market and choose to pursue the career prospects that fit into my projected results. Most importantly, I was no longer embarrassed about where I was working and how long it was taking me to receive a job offer in the corporate world; I was the only one who was qualified to determine my pace and that was now no longer influenced by the velocity of my peers.

In late May, the Spoleto Festival brought tons of tourists to downtown Charleston. I was ineligible for the weekend drawings since I had won during the Bridge Run. One Friday we were slammed. Phones were ringing off the hook, guests were piling in and my manager had gone home sick. I stepped in to try to organize the chaos and had to wear many hats in the process. As I had a phone to my ear inputting a wake-up call and simultaneously typing in the dates of arrival in our system for the person that was on hold to see if we had any rooms for the following weekend while still being forced to nod yes or no to questions from my co-worker who had just started two days earlier, a guest approached the counter and said "Does this hotel not have bellman anymore?"

By that time I finished inputting the wake-up call and was waiting for the screen to load to indicate if we had rooms. "Yes sir we do," I said "has no one come to help you?"

"I haven't even seen a bellman walk through this lobby in the last 15 minutes", he said. "I would do it myself, but I can't even find a cart and I would rather not make 10 trips."

"I understand sir," I said, "if you give me one moment I'll be right with you."

I picked up the phone and told the lady that was waiting that we were all booked for the dates she requested and asked if I could transfer her to central reservations to check any additional dates. She was fine with that so I transferred her and went around the counter to help the gentleman who had just complained.

"I'm sorry again that you had to wait, Mister...."

"Owen, Franklin Owen" he said.

I went and found a cart myself and proceeded to follow him to the curb to unload his car. He had several bags and what appeared to be a projector screen along with an easel. "Are you doing a presentation here?" I asked. He said, "Yes, I'm presenting to one of our largest customers in the area and want to make sure that I am completely prepared. That's why I'm hauling all of this stuff up to my room, I'll probably practice seven or eight times tonight." I asked him who he worked for as we waited on the elevator to arrive. "Canvass," he said. I had never heard of the company and had no clue of what they did; I decided not to ask so that I didn't badger a guest with questions so I just said ok.

"Ever heard of us?" he asked.

"No Sir", I said and he smiled and said "Most people haven't." He went on to tell me that they were a small Regional company that worked with large customers. At Canvass, their vision was to help companies establish or improve their image in the market place. They had been around for many years but their name was often a lot more private than their remarkable public work. When we arrived on the fifth floor, we walked down to room 517; I opened the door and began to unload all of his luggage.

When I finished I asked if there was anything else that I could do to assist him and he said "Not at all, you've been great." He pulled out a hand full of cash and released his money clip to locate the specific bill to tip me. "No thank you," I said, "I appreciate the gesture, but I am also sorry that you had to wait." I informed him that his wait was not the normal level of service that our establishment found acceptable and hoped that his stay would be exceptional from this point forward. He reached out and gave me a handshake and I left the room. By the time I reached room 511, I heard a voice say "Young man." I turned and it was Mr. Owen. He handed me a business card and said, "If you ever decide that you'd like to pursue a career outside of the hotel industry, please give me a call."

"Thank you," I said as my mind raced, attempting to process what was taking place. I placed his business card in my wallet and proceeded to get back downstairs to make it through the rush. By 11 p.m., everything was calm and my shift was over. I headed back home instead of heading to the normal gathering spots in the market due to exhaustion. When I got home and showered, I was ready to crash and then I remembered what I had put in my wallet. I pulled the business card out and went to the company's website to see what they were all about. As I read the company history, mission statement, vision statement and core values, I reached inside my portfolio and pulled out the napkins that I had written on during my talk with Professor Humbert. That night I started to assess whether Canvass met the criteria for my *T.O.W.E.R.*

On that Sunday, I went to church for the first time in a couple of weeks. I was running a little behind but planned to sit in the balcony like I normally did. To my surprise, the service was packed that day and I ended up having to sit in a fold out chair directly in front of the pulpit. I had never sat that close in church before. Because I was late, the choir was standing to sing their final song right before the Pastor stood up to preach. The soloist sang 'God *is Trying to Tell You Something*" and was just as good, if not better, than the artist on the sound track; I really enjoyed it. After the song, Pastor Dogan stood up and read his opening scripture. His subject was in the form of a question, "What is God Trying to Tell You?" During the message I listened more intently than I normally did, potentially due to the fact that I was unable to do a periodic text message check because I was sitting so close. As he approached the end of his message, he said something that caught my attention. He said, "Just like God did for Noah, He will provide you with the blueprints to build whatever structure is necessary to endure your journey. What is it that you're trying to build today? Whatever it is, just know that God will often use unexpected encounters to help you along the way." I pondered those words all the way home and decided that I would attempt to meet with Mr. Owen before he left town.

I called him on that Sunday, hoping to get his voicemail but he answered, "Franklin Owen," he said.

"I'm sorry Sir, I was expecting to get your voicemail and leave you a message, I really didn't mean to bother you on a Sunday!" I said.

"Who am I speaking with?" he asked.

"Sorry," I said, "This is Warren Nichols from the hotel, you gave me your card the other day and said that I should call if I was interested in a career change. I was hoping to have a chance to speak with you before you leave town, but I totally understand if you're too busy."

By this time he can clearly tell that I'm flustered and says, "Warren, I would love to talk with you. Do you have dinner plans tonight?"

"No sir," I said. He told me to meet him in the hotel lobby at 6:15 and we would decide on a place to eat then. He told me to bring him a copy of my resume as well. I was so excited and nervous at the same time; so much that I went back and forth 10 times on what to wear. I finally called Sam to come over and together we picked out a suitable shirt and tie combination.

I arrived at the hotel at 5:45pm. I decided to sit in the coffee shop across the street to avoid running into co-workers and having to answer 100 questions as to why I was there. At five after six, I waited in the lobby. Mr. Owen stepped off the elevator at 6:15 sharp, shook my hand and said "You hungry?"

"Yes sir" I said and we walked down to Meeting Street to find a place to eat. After we ordered, he asked me how much I knew about the company. I went over the details that I had learned from researching the website and then he filled in the gaps with his version of the company's profile along with the story of how he was hired. After he finished, I asked what position was open and he said, "We need a D.I.T. in the Charleston office." He said that the Charleston office had just opened a few years earlier and they were now experiencing growth and expansion. Though I had reviewed their website, I hadn't seen any openings or job descriptions that gave me a clue of what a D.I.T was. So I asked, "What is a D.I.T.?"

He laughed and said, "Forgive me for speaking in acronyms. A *D.I.T.* is a *Dreamer In Training*," he said. "Our company has a unique way of creating job titles; the goal is to provide clarity to our employees as to their purpose as well as to our customers regarding the service that we provide to them," he said.

We went on to talk about my background and experience along with what my goals were in life. He told me that the position was one that they planned to fill immediately and what it paid, which was a few thousand dollars more than what I made at the hotel. After dessert, the waiter told us that he would be right back with our check. While we waited, Mr. Owen looked me square in the eyes and said "Warren would you like to dream with us?" Without hesitation I said, "Yes, I would love to!" He reached across the table, shook my hand and said, "I will have our HR Department contact you tomorrow to complete the necessary paperwork and to extend you an official offer."

Points to Ponder

- The speed of others shouldn't dictate your pace.
- **T.O.W.E.R.**
  1. Is pursuing this job opening a decision that is *Tactical?*
  2. Does this role provide me with *Options?*

3. Have I determined for myself what I am *Worth*?
4. Is this a transitionary opportunity or a place where I can be *Embedded*?
5. Does this opportunity add value to my projected *Results*?

"...the tower is built high in order to assist in supporting other materials, therefore, we cannot become fixated on the highest point of the tower because the tower is not the portion of the bridge on which you stand."

4
THE ABUTMENT

IT WAS ALMOST too good to be true as I sat in the parking lot of the office park and looked up at the office windows. Which one would be mine I wondered as I waited until 7:45 to get out of the car because walking in at 7 a.m. when I arrived may seem a bit too eager. When I walked in the front door, I told the switchboard operator that my name was Warren Nichols. She smiled and said, "Nice to meet you, how can I help you?" I quickly realized that she ran the switch board for the entire building and had no clue why I was there at all. I tried to save face by telling her that I just wanted to say hello and made my way to the wall to view the directory.

Canvass was located on the 3rd floor, which was actually the first one up since the parking garage was below the lobby. When I stepped off the elevator I walked down the hall to Suite 316. When I walked in I was greeted by the office coordinator, "You must be Warren," she said, "I'm Virginia; welcome to Canvass!"

She showed me to my desk that was located in a corner in a cubical area with three other people. After meeting Rory, Marc and Charly, it was clear that we would be spending a lot of time together. They told me that collectively we were known as the Dream Team and that it was our job to synergize to develop creative concepts for our customers. Rory was the L.D., which stood for Lead Dreamer, Marc was the C.D., which stood for Certified Dreamer and Charly and I were both D.I.T's; she had just started one month before me. The first week went by slowly as I spent most of my time reading S.O.P.'s, completing on-line training and shadowing Virginia at the Front Desk. Everyone at Canvass had to understand the operation from the ground up before they were allowed to work on anything.

That Friday, Franklin returned to the office and I attended my first staff meeting. It was a meeting filled with big announcements as we were informed that we were *Office of the Month* for the company. We had just landed a huge account and that due to the growth our office, we would now have a local C.O.D. instead of Franklin managing everything regionally. The entire office applauded as Rory was named the Coordinator of Dreams. Evidently he had been with the company only nine months and was on the fast track. Franklin said, "Rory's promotion is a testament to the fact that Canvass is built upon hard work. It doesn't matter where you've come from or how long you've been here, if you are dedicated, you'll be successful." After the meeting, Rory and Franklin talked for a long time in his office. While I was reading through the two accounts that I would be training on, I glanced over and saw Marc's resume on his screen. He minimized the screen when he saw me look and I pretended not to see it. Throughout the rest of the day as Rory moved his stuff into Franklin's old office, Marc had a lot of calls on his cell phone and conducted several coded conversations.

At 5, everyone shut down their computers and prepared for the weekend. Rory announced that he was buying drinks for everyone at the pub around the corner; the entire office went out to celebrate with him. After a couple of hours I was ready to head home. When I got up to leave, Charly followed me to my car. She asked for my cell phone number and gave me hers and said she'd see me Monday. On Saturday afternoon, she called me and said that we needed to talk. She wanted me to know that Marc was livid over the fact that Rory had been promoted due to the fact that Marc had been with the company since they opened the Charleston location five years ago. She said that Marc told her that he had updated his resume and was going to quit as soon as he received an offer.

Although I tried not to say much, my mind raced with tons of questions. Why hadn't Marc been promoted yet? Why was Rory moving up so fast? Did Rory know that Marc was angry? Did the two of them get along? Did Franklin know about any of this? Why had Marc aired all of his dirty laundry with Charly? What did Charly think about it after being with the company for only a month? Should I already be looking for another job? How would the tensions be on Monday? In spite of knowing what I shouldn't,

I asked Charly every one of those questions. She answered half of them on the phone and the other half at a restaurant on King Street after being on the phone for two hours and then realizing that we had ventured into the same area.

According to Charly, Marc and Franklin never really hit it off due to the fact that Marc made a snide remark in front of a customer to Franklin regarding Carolina beating Clemson for the past few years. Marc was insistent that Franklin could dish it out but couldn't take it and never really got over it. Rory on the other hand was Franklin's *"Golden Child"*, due to the fact that Rory represented a true dreamer in Franklin's eyes. I learned that Rory was the product of two parents who both did drugs prior to and during his conception. He spent most of his childhood in orphanages and was homeless at 17 as a Senior in high school. He entered an oratorical contest that was sponsored by a local scholarship committee and Franklin was asked to judge. Rory's speech was based on his life and caused the judges and everyone else in the room to cry during a standing ovation. From that day on, Franklin never stopped keeping up with Rory's progress and met him after he graduated from the Citadel to offer him a job. Nine months later Rory is the C.O.D.

Charly said that she likes Canvass, but noticed that there weren't many women in leadership. She had no interest in moving any further than a C.O.D. due to the fact that she was taking the LSAT and planning to attend Law School part-time while she worked. She really liked Virginia and Franklin but was worried about the drama that would take place on Monday. She really liked Marc and Rory but perceived that Marc was much more knowledgeable about the company. She also feels that Rory has a lot of talent but no true understanding of our business, at least that's what Marc would always say. She wasn't bias at all of course and the fact that she and Marc's girlfriend pledged the same sorority and were roommates in college had nothing to do with her views.

Needless to say after lunch on Saturday, I was all confused. I wasn't sure if I had made the right decision or not in light of all that had taken place during my first week. On Monday, I was nervous as I entered the office. Ironically the day was very uneventful. Charly and I spent time training with Marc on the details of our new account but no one said a word about what had transpired or what we feared would eventually happen with Marc leaving.

A month later Marc was still there and it was time to launch the project for the new account that we had landed during my first week. Over the last month Charly and I talked a couple of times a week about the office and the dynamics and sad to say ,I had slipped into a habit of "after-hours gossip". Charly was now a C.O.D. and Marc was the L.D.; I was still a D.I.T. and had a little more training to complete before I earned my first stripes. That morning, Franklin came to the office along with Cheryl who was the corporate Administrative Assistant. After they came in and greeted everyone, Rory announced that the Charleston office would be taking a field trip. To my surprise we drove out to the harbor and boarded a boat. During the boat ride we all enjoyed the cool breeze; no one asked where we were headed. Once we arrived at a spot close to the Cooper River Bridge, Rory asked the Captain to turn the engine off. He took us all up to the front of the boat and asked, "Do you guys know what that's called?" He pointed at a spot near the bridge and Marc spoke up sarcastically and said "Ummm, I think it's a bridge."

"Good answer", Rory said with an enormous smile, "however that's not exactly the answer that I'm looking for. Anyone else?" He looked for a willing soul. When no one answered he explained, "The portion of the bridge that I was pointing to is called the Abutment.

The Abutment is the part of the bridge that holds up the ends of the deck. Over the past month a lot of transition has taken place in our operation. Some of you agree with things and some of you don't. I can tell by the obvious frustrations a few of the things that have taken place have left some of you feeling slighted and others fearful of what might happen next. It's been difficult to even have an in-office conversation due to the fact that I'm sure some or all of you have discussed this outside of the office daily. So why are we here? We are here because I need your support. We are about to embark on one of the largest projects our company has ever obtained. There were conversations around whether we should even be allowed to manage this account since most of us are so new. On the day I was promoted, Franklin told me that the company was considering relocating a team of seasoned veterans from corporate to handle this project. He said he realized that due to the transition, we may have a hard time gaining the necessary cohesiveness needed to successfully achieve the outcomes that we promised our new client. I told him on that day that I appreciated his concern but I felt we deserved the opportunity. I convinced him that day, in spite of what we may encounter emotionally, I believe this group will support me. I realize that I am only as good as the team that I have supporting me, therefore, I'm asking you today to make the sacrifice of being my Abutment. It's a sacrifice because this portion of a bridge is never truly recognized for its efforts. As a matter of fact, during construction, the celebration is directed more towards the fact that this portion indicates a closeness of completion more than an appreciation for its actual function. I want it to be clear to each of you today that I know your value and if you are willing, we'll leave all of our challenges out here in the river and return as a team. If you accept and agree then we'll govern ourselves by the *S.T.A.N.D. Concept* moving forward and I promise you, the sky is the limit."

When he finished everyone was silent for at least three minutes. Marc stood up first and said, "I'm in!" The rest of us followed, including Sharon who was the newest member of our team. We all embraced each other and you could feel the sense of excitement as the boat took us back to the dock. When we arrived back at the office, we all were ready to hit the ground running and prepared vigorously for our staff meeting that would start after lunch. Before we could get started, Sharon stopped Rory in the cubicle area and asked him, "What is the *S.T.A.N.D. Concept?*" I was relieved because I thought that I was the only one that didn't know but it turned out that no one knew. Rory was elated that Sharon asked and invited us all into the conference room. When we got there, he wrote on the board:

1. *Speak* to each other when obstacles arise.
2. *Together* we can resolve any issue.
3. *Accept* constructive criticism from anyone, regardless of title.
4. *Never* allow an uninvolved team member to be pulled into or to enter into conflict.
5. *Dedicate* ourselves to fighting with, instead of against, each other.

When he finished, we all agreed that we would *S.T.A.N.D.* as a team. It reminded me of all of the conversations Charly and I had that tore the team apart vs. bringing unity. I felt bad for allowing Charly's opinions of people to shape my own and realized that over the last month I hadn't invested any time getting to know any of them for myself. Charly had shaped my perception of the entire company. After work that day I told Charly that we would have to start our relationship over. I was serious about fully adhering to our pact to *S.T.A.N.D.* and didn't want anything to circumvent that process. Surprisingly she agreed and apologized for any part she played in the drama that had taken place in our office over that last month. This was an exciting time, it felt like I was starting a new job with a new company all over again.

The next two and a half years were amazing. Marc became the new A.C.O.D. which was a position that Rory convinced Franklin to create due to the complete 180 that Marc had the day after our boat trip. Marc was now happy to allow his knowledge and expertise to serve as a support system for the team instead of with- holding his experience because of feeling slighted. This made us a great team and resulted in a bitter sweet outcome. Marc was asked to relocate to Savannah to expand the business as the C.O.D. over that location. Franklin was promoted to V.P.O.D. which meant that now his and Marc's positions were open. Everyone in the company knew from Charleston to Charlotte that Rory would be offered Franklin's position but the question was, what would happen then? I planned to apply for the A.C.O.D. position but never got a chance to. Rory asked me to have dinner with him after work one Monday and told me that Sharon had been promoted into that position. I was thankful at that moment that he had given us the Abutment example and taught us the *S.T.A.N.D. Concept*; it helped me actually get over all my initial emotions during the appetizer and not choke on my food. While we waited on the entrée, he informed me that a lot was going to change in our office. The first change he wanted to discuss was asking me to be the C.O.D., which would mean assuming his position. I was shocked, overjoyed and honored at the same time. He told me that my work had proven me to be a great leader and that he knew I would do a great job! "This is exciting," I replied with excitement, "so now you can move into Franklin's prior role as the R.D.O.C. and we can still work together."

He smiled and said, "Yes and no."

He told me that he was sure that we would still work together in some capacity but that the company had decided to make some Regional adjustments in hopes of sparking some new collaborations and ensuring that we continue to be competitive as we pursue our goal of becoming a market leader in our industry. As a result, this meant that Franklin was moving to the corporate office in Columbia, Rory was moving to the Atlanta Region and I would have a new boss who was being hired from outside of the company from one of our leading competitors; his name was Edward Boyles and he came with very high expectations.

Over the next month, all of the announcements were made and for the following six months, we transitioned into our new structure. After several celebratory and going away gatherings, we now had a new team. I was the C.O.D., Sharon was the A.C.O.D., Virginia had been given the opportunity to move up and train and was now the L.D., Charly was still there as a C.D. but was half-way through Law School and our two new team members were Richard who was a C.D. ,Elaina who was a D.I.T. and also spoke fluent Spanish and Beth who was our new Office Coordinator. Everything had seemingly fallen into place. I was now in a management role after only three years with the company. I began to reflect on my bridge and discovered that I now had three major parts. College had been my *FIRM FOUNDATION*. Choosing a career field represented my *TOWER* and with the help of Rory, I now knew what an *ABUTMENT* was and had spent three years in a support role to my team; I was really proud of how far I had come. It was a weekend of festivity as I had dinner with my family and friends and began hunting for a house. All that was left to do was to meet my new boss Edward Boyles on Monday morning.

Points to Ponder

- Never allow the opinions of others to shape your perceptions.

- We all have to be willing to serve as an *ABUTMENT* to support others if we'll ever truly lead.
- **S.T.A.N.D.**
  1. *Speak* to each other when obstacles arise.
  2. *Together* we can resolve any issue.
  3. *Accept* constructive criticism from anyone regardless of title.
  4. *Never* allow an uninvolved team member to be pulled into or to enter into conflict.
  5. *Dedicate* ourselves to fighting with instead of against each other.

"...make the sacrifice of being my Abutment. It's a sacrifice because this portion of a bridge is never truly recognized for its efforts. As a matter of fact, during construction, the celebration is directed more towards the fact that this portion indicates a closeness of completion more than an appreciation for its actual function."

5
THE SUSPENSION CABLES

ON MONDAY, I decided to stop and pick up doughnuts and coffee for my team. I was excited about my new role and knew that I had to take every opportunity to show them how much they're appreciated for their hard work and support. When I arrived at the office, everyone was pleasantly surprised about the early morning treat. Around 9:15, I heard Beth in the cubicle area asking Virginia to cover the Front Desk for a moment. When she returned, she was walking behind a gentleman in a three-piece suit who wore shades. When they entered the office, I heard her introducing him as Mr. Boyles and asking where he would like her to place his bags. He asked if the conference room was being occupied and she said no. I gathered my things to head towards the conference room to introduce myself and saw him handing Beth his coat.

"Good Morning", I said, "I'm Warren and you must be Edward, nice to meet you!".

"Mr. Boyles", he said as he shook my hand. As Beth headed out of the room he said, "Do you guys have coffee around here?".

"Yes sir," she said.

"Good," he said, "I take it black with one pack of sugar."

As Beth left the room I attempted to gather myself before we moved on. I asked him what his agenda was for the day and how long he'd be in town that week. He told me that due to the size of the Charleston market, he had convinced Franklin that he needed to be stationed there and just travel to the other locations. As a result, he would be turning the conference room into his office and we could schedule to use the conference room with the switch board operator as needed. "Oh", I said, "I wasn't made aware of this."

"This was an Executive Level decision", he said. "We've been discussing it for the last six months during my company orientation. The movers will be here tomorrow with my furniture. In the meantime, why don't you introduce me to the support staff and then you and I will catch up after that."

"I would be glad to introduce you to the team," I said as I walked out to the Dream Team area. I went around the room and introduced each person and gave a brief summary of their company history as well as their current duties. When I finished, I then introduced Mr. Boyles along with informing everyone that he would be stationed in our former conference room. "Now I will turn the floor over to our newest Regional Coordinator of Dreams, Edward Boyles." The group applauded as he prepared to speak.

"I won't be long today," he said. "Let me just say that it's good to meet all of you. And though I'll be here in this office, most of my interactions will not be with your level, therefore, you should still communicate all of your needs to Warren and he will report the details back to me for my approval or denial. I am aware that many of you are accustomed to being on a first name basis with leadership, and though I want to ensure you that I am available to you if need be, I find it most appropriate if you refer to me as Mr. Boyles. I hear that there are a lot of good things going on here at Canvass and it is my belief that after the next few months of us working together, I can guide you into turning those good things into great things. Thank you for your time and attention."

When he finished, he asked Elaina to follow us down the hall. When the three of us walked in the conference room he said, "Did you say that you were fluent in Spanish?"

"Yes", she said, "I've been bi-lingual all my life."

"That's awesome," he said, "my wife is fluent and always gives me a hard time for not knowing two words. Here's a number to a local florist that I use, send her an arrangement of lilies to this address and tell her that I'm always thinking of her, in Spanish. That'll be all, thanks," he said.

When Elaina left the room I was very quiet, for the next hour he ran down all of his accolades and awards over his 11 year career in the image consulting industry. He told me that he really had to think long and hard prior to joining an organization like ours. He was accustomed to traveling the entire globe every 90 days and previously held a role of Regional V.P. The titles at Canvass were an issue for him but his wife insisted on being more stable for the children, as their son was starting the ninth grade. Canvass was more convincing with their checkbook than they were the title and due to the stock that he'd cashed in when he left his prior company, it really was unnecessary for him to work; the drive inside of him to mentor and develop up-and-coming leaders like me was too strong to sit back. He knew that it was meant for him to take people who had raw talent like me and mold us with the exposure that he'd been privileged to have.

By the time we finished, he asked if I was free for lunch and I told him that I had a previously scheduled meeting. "That's fine", he said, "I need to get a work-out in anyway. I'll see you back here in an hour then," he said. "It may take me a little longer, but I'm sure your work won't allow you to take lunches any longer than that," he said, "but feel free if there's ever a need. All work and no play isn't good for anyone," he said. As I got onto the elevator to head down to the parking garage, I couldn't even look into the glass mirror. I drove over to a local park and sat on the bench for an hour. Charly called my cell phone and texted me to see how the initial meeting went; I didn't respond to either message and just sat in silence the entire time. I was literally wondering if I'd been selected for an episode of Punk'd. I mean this guy has Beth meet him outside to get his bags, has her fetch him coffee, makes Elaina order flowers in Spanish, tells us all to call him Mr. Boyles and then basically tells me and my entire team how fortunate we are to have him here!!!!! "God, please tell me that I am imagining all of this and that I'm going to wake up and it will soon be over!" Unfortunately, when I got back to the office he was still there. There were no TV producers yelling *'gotcha'* and I spent the next three hours walking him through our metrics and client profiles. I was then asked to schedule the appropriate level meetings with all our clients for him within the next two weeks

"Appropriate level?" I asked.

"Yes." he said. "What I mean is that there are some people that you need to meet with at your level and others that I need to focus on at mine. If you're unsure just ask me prior to scheduling. Okay, I think we've hit it pretty hard for the day, be sure to send me some notes to recap our meeting. I'll plan to review them tonight."

I went back to my office and sat at my desk and stared out of the window. "I tried to call you" Charly said as she stood in the door. I told her that it had been a very busy day and that we'd catch up tomorrow. I know that she had to see the disgust on my face so I turned back and looked out of the window as she left. I stayed for another hour to type up the notes and to begin scheduling the meetings that Edward, I mean, Mr. Boyles had requested.

The next morning, I told myself during my morning shave that this would be a better day. I needed to give Mr. Boyles the benefit of the doubt and not allow a few things that rubbed me the wrong way to cause us to get off on the wrong foot. That lasted until about 7:45 when I received a text on the way to the office.

"Let Beth know that I'll be pulling up around 8:15, also will you thank Evelyn for ordering those flowers, my wife was thrilled. Thanks, MB." I was thankful that no one was next to me because I literally swerved into the other lane. Who did this guy think that he was? He's turning Beth into a personal assistant, he can't even remember Elaina's name and now he's texting me his initials for Mr. Boyles!!!!

I wish that I could tell you that the next seven months were better but they actually grew worse. He seemingly second guessed and critiqued my every effort and while the team was still productive and breaking records, they could see the pressure wearing on me. I don't know which part was worse; was it the fact that he treated the staff as if they were unworthy of even speaking to him or was it the way he took the credit for all of our success? Anytime that our leadership team came for a visit it was "I told Warren this", "I'm working with him on that", "With a little more work, he'll be a strong asset", "Warren is really responding to my tutelage." It seemed that Franklin and George Benson, our Chief Dreaming Officers were believing every word he said. The truth was that our clients hated him because he spoke to them like they were beneath him. The morale in our office was at an all-time low because everyone had to cater to Caesar and I don't know when he had the time to impart so much wisdom into me because I didn't play golf or trade the stock market which he did all day when he wasn't criticizing me.

One Sunday, I asked Pastor Dogan if I could meet with him after service. I shared briefly with him the struggles I was having, after informing him it was his sermon that motivated me to pursue this company. We had a very pleasant talk and I told him that I was thinking of sending my resume out to some companies; he told me that he would be praying that I make the right decision. On my way out of his office I said "Well, I guess I'm going to have to rebuild my bridge."

"Rebuild?" as he looked confused. I then told him about how Professor Humbert had taken me to the bridge in college and how I still equated so many of my career lessons and goals to building a bridge. He seemed very excited and asked if I was headed home right away. I told him that I had a few minutes and he asked me to meet him outside in 10 minutes. When he came out, he asked me if I would take a ride with him. As you may have guessed, we headed towards the Cooper River Bridge. When we got to where we could see it clearly, he pulled to the side of East Bay Street. We got out and he said, "Do you know what they call those things that are connected to the tower?"

"No sir," I said.

He went on to explain, "Those are called Suspension Cables. Suspension Cables are the tension members of a bridge that hang from the tower and are ultimately connected to the main deck on which we drive. In order to get from the tower to the deck, there has to be a lot of tension and pressure placed on the cables. If you're building a bridge, you have to realize that it's going to cost you something. Now you could walk away from the Mr. Boyles' of the world, but if you do, you'll miss a very necessary element of your journey. In life there will always be people who come along to test us and sometimes push us to the edge, however, the tension and the pressure is actually placed in our lives to make us stronger. Listen, I know the workplace is often viewed as a place where you have to *'go along to get along'* but I believe that you can still *F.I.G.H.T.* Do you know what I mean when I say *F.I.G.H.T.*?"

I shook my head so I wouldn't to have to speak as I held back the tears. This was the first time that I had ever shared my concerns with anyone. I had planned to leave without saying anything to make sure that I didn't break my commitment to

Rory to *S.T.A.N.D.* Pastor Dogan had now helped me understand I didn't have to accept unjust leadership. I can *F.I.G.H.T.* I wrote the meaning of the letters on a Subway napkin that he had in his car:

1. *Focus* on what you can control.
2. *Inspire* the team around you.
3. *Give* your best effort daily.
4. *Handle* adversity with a smile.
5. *Take* the opportunity to expose the truth when it comes.

After our conversation that Sunday, I realized I had thrown in the towel on my team. The pressure from Mr. Boyles was so great that I had given up on trying to be a leader. The truth is that I had been reduced to nothing more than just one of his assistants. That Monday, I took on a new attitude. I had a staff meeting for the first time in three months and told my team that we had to return to being that, a team! Over the next two months, I went back to being a better leader than I was to begin with. I started sending emails randomly to employees who were performing well, even though Mr. Boyles advised against it. I started taking people to lunch again even though he limited me to one person per month to ensure we watched the bottom line; I then decided to take someone different twice a week and pay for the expenses out of my own pocket. Although it drove him crazy, we started yelling and dancing in the office again when someone had a great idea. I started inviting employees over to my house for BBQ's again, even though I was instructed not to fraternize with the '*help*'. I was able to get Beth out of being a courier and a waitress by assigning her to do client drop-ins most mornings and on the mornings that there were no clients to see, the phones were always "extremely busy" and I convinced Mr. Boyles that no one else was available to fill her role. He eventually left Elaina alone after she "mistakenly" sent flowers to his wife and said "*I love you Sally*", instead of *Justine*. Ironically, he didn't want her sending his wife flowers any more. Although I had re-energized my team, Mr. Boyles increased his pressure on me. It seemed as though he discredited me every chance he got as if he feared I would get more '*at-a-boys*' than him.

One Friday I was reviewing my notes from my conversation with Pastor Dogan while I was on a plane headed to Napa Valley for a week. It appeared as though everything was working except for the last part. When I returned from a week of relaxation, I returned to chaos. I had turned my phone off for the last two days of vacation and had 43 messages when I returned. Most of them were from Mr. Boyles and one was from Charly. As soon as I finished clearing them, Charly beeped in. She said that she knew I didn't want to hear any gossip but I needed to be ready for a meeting that was happening first thing Monday morning with Mr. Boyles, Franklin and George regarding our financial reports. Evidently, there were billing discrepancies on an invoice during the week that I was gone and our largest customer called corporate to complain. The reason they felt the need to call corporate is because Mr. Boyles told them that if he didn't receive payment that week and we would not run their latest press release that was slated to go out that Friday.

Although their invoice was wrong, they felt forced to pay it and were now demanding a refund, an apology and someone's head on a platter. On that Monday, I realized that Mr. Boyles intended for that person to be me. He stood in his office and berated me in front of Franklin and George for my incompetence and stated that he had been trying to mentor me but that I was learning too slow. Even though I wanted to scream, I smiled and asked if I could be excused for a moment. When I returned I asked him if he could show me where I had made the mistake. I hooked the laptop up to the projector so that the entire room could see. Mr. Boyles turned completely red as he struggled to log on to our Intranet System. Once he finally logged in, he was unable to locate the client, their invoice or any information regarding the issue that he'd been mentoring me on. It was clear that Franklin and George were shocked and that's when I took the floor.

I went into my email account and found the 10 emails I sent him prior to my vacation, all of which were explanations of basic processes and procedures that I learned during my time as a D.I.T. One of those emails included very specific details as to how to handle matters with the customer that had complained. I pointed out that I even called the customer prior to my departure and informed them that I'd be unavailable but Mr. Boyles would be their point of contact. After I finished, Franklin and George asked if I'd excuse myself. Later that afternoon, after the smoke cleared, they asked if they could speak with me. They let me know that Mr. Boyles had blown up during the meeting and stormed out after quitting; they wanted to apologize for his behavior during the meeting. It was a long afternoon as I recounted what the last nine months had been like in our office. They took notes and asked to speak with the rest of the staff one-on-one. They vowed to get back with me regarding what had taken place and to discuss next steps for the opening that Mr. Boyles resignation created.

That evening I rode home slowly across the Cooper River Bridge and found myself in tears again as I stared up at the Suspension Cables. I had been pulled and stretched beyond any limits I'd ever expected, but yet, my bridge was still standing.

Points to Ponder

- We will often be tested by the transitions in our environment.
- Quitting under pressure will cause us to miss out on a valuable and necessary lesson.
- *F.I.G.H.T.*
  1. *Focus* on what you can control.
  2. *Inspire* the team around you.
  3. *Give* your best effort daily.
  4. *Handle* adversity with a smile.
  5. *Take* the opportunity to expose the truth when it comes.

"...in order to get from the tower to the deck, there has to be a lot of tension and pressure placed on the cables. If you're building a bridge, you have to realize that it's going to cost you something."

6
THE DECK

I COULDN'T BELIEVE that I was being promoted to Regional Coordinator of Dreams after only four years with the company. I was so excited that I posted pictures of my new business cards online so all my friends could see. Now it was time to ensure that we were prepared for growth in the coming year; I now had to fill my previous position and complete a forecast for the next twelve months. I decided to post the position in the office instead of hand-picking anyone. To my surprise, everyone expressed interest, which opened a door that I hadn't expected. By being able to spend time with each person, I was able to gain insight and innovative ideas from each of them as to what they would do if they were leading the entire team. Often, we miss out on the benefit of a diverse perspective due to our innate desire to have people conform to our thoughts. I mean who would of thought that Beth, who had only experienced our clients from a customer service standpoint, would have so many impressive ideas regarding continuous improvement and new service offerings. I realized that day that although I had developed a strong and highly productive team, I had unintentionally robbed them of some of their individualism. Even when I realized how much they had to offer, I'll admit that I was still a little uneasy. Some of the things that they suggested were outside of my comfort zone, therefore, in order for us to move forward, I would have to relinquish more control than I was used to and embrace them as *"the-subject-matter-expert"*. As uneasy as it made me feel, I knew deep down that this was the right way to go.

After all of the interviews, I chose Sharon to be the new C.O.D., Elaina became the new A.C.O.D, Virginia remained the L.D., Richard and Charly were still C.D.'s, Beth was promoted to a D.I.T. and our newest team member Brett became the Office Coordinator. It was getting close to Thanksgiving and Christmas which meant all of the managers had to submit their budgets and business plans for the following year. I worked with Sharon and we made a very bold decision; instead of her and me driving to Corporate to do the presentation, we decided to invite George, Franklin and Bill Dalton, our CFO, to Charleston. It was an easy sell since everyone is always eager to get to the coast but they were in for a surprise; the presentation was going to be a lot different this time. I called a local staffing company to get some Front Desk help for the day so that when they arrived at the building's Executive Conference Room, our entire team would be in attendance. I opened the meeting by thanking them for coming and asking that they keep an open mind throughout our presentation. I began to cover the previous year's budget, Sharon covered the previous year's metrics and then it was time to discuss business plans. We started with Beth whose topic was *'Building a Gate'* that they'll travel to see. She used the analogy of the wrought iron gates that Phillip Simmons made and how people came from miles around to see his work. She felt that by continuously improving the way our Office Coordinator's company-wide serviced our customers, others would flock just to see how we serve. She also felt that we could then create a new service that offered image consulting specifically for Customer Service Departments within our client base. Elaina was next and she opened by saying, "Lienzo es una impresionante organización que construye relaciones con grandes empresas, como hablan el mismo idioma." Translated that means, "Canvass is an awesome organization that builds relationships with great companies, as long as they speak the same language." She continued in English to express the need for Canvass to expand their business mix to more diverse companies due to the immense growth in the Hispanic business community. Richard came next and spoke about how there was an opportunity to consult individual Veterans who are transitioning into the civilian population and he expressed how hard it was for him to adjust to the differences in military vs. civilian operations. Virginia highlighted how we should review our own image; she noted that it would be remiss for us to *"dress our customers in tuxedos while we wear overalls"*.

Charly gave a more personal plea as she spoke about her love for Canvass and how becoming an Attorney shouldn't be the end of her career with the company, but only the beginning. She felt that she could assist the company with breaking into the legal profession and consulting them in a number of ways. As a result of Brett being brand new, he was the only one that didn't present, however, I wanted him to be a part of the meeting in order to ensure that he felt like a valued member of the team. Once the presentations were done, Sharon and I presented the new budget and how we planned to incorporate all of their ideas. After the meeting, I went to lunch with George, Franklin and Bill. We hadn't discussed the meeting yet so I was anxious to see how they felt. Once we were seated, George said, "I have been with this company for 25 years and have never attended a meeting like this, you really should have told us that you were going to do this!" My stomach dropped as I took a big gulp of my water.

All of a sudden, Franklin burst into laughter and George hit him on the shoulder. Franklin apologized for not being able to keep a straight face and they all began to laugh. They had huddled up after the meeting and all planned to scare me to death by making me think I was in big trouble. On the contrary, they loved the idea and they were very impressed that we took the risk to present in that way. Needless to say, it turned out to be a great lunch meeting.

The next year flew by and before I could blink, it was already October and we were all busy trying to complete everything before Thanksgiving. The Charleston Office of Canvass had grown by 67% in a single year and we had so many clients and potential customers beating our door down, we decided to purchase our own building. Virginia was so happy we were now *'dressing ourselves up'*. I received a call that day from George with some excited yet unsettling news. They wanted me to speak at the End-of-the-Year Manager's Meeting on a topic of my choice based on the growth that we'd experienced in the past year; they were interested in the projections for the next three years. I was honored when I realized that I was now the youngest manager who would be attending the meeting and speaking to guys that I had admired and sought out for advice my entire career with the company. Even though I was proud of the work that I'd done, I wasn't a Public Speaker and didn't have any clue as to how to formally explain to anyone how we'd been so successful.

With the meeting only two weeks away in Columbia, I immediately starting racking my mind as to what I would say. I went back over the presentation that we did last year this time but I couldn't bring the entire team to Columbia. I started flipping back through some of the leadership books I'd read over the years but didn't find anything that sparked any ideas; I went home that day with my mind racing. I stopped at Subway on the way home since I was in no mood to cook and when the guy handed me the bag at the second window, it hit me. I remembered the conversation that I'd had with Pastor Dogan that helped me through my issue with Mr. Boyles. When I got home I looked in my desk and there it was, the Subway napkin with *F.I.G.H.T.* on it along with my notepad that had *S.T.A.N.D.* on it from Rory's boat trip along with the napkins that had *T.O.W.E.R.* on them from the Bridge Run conversation with Professor Humbert. After I found all of that, I opened the box where I kept all of my college mementos. I pulled out the spiral notebook that had *M.O.V.E.* written in it. I realized that everything I needed was right in front of me and perhaps I needed to drive myself to the bridge now to gather my thoughts. When I got to the parking lot, there was another guy sitting in his car. I got out and walked over to the gate and began to stare up at the bridge. I heard a door slam and as I looked back, he was walking over. "It's a shame that they're going to tear these bridges down and build a new one huh?" he said. They had already started construction on the new bridge.

"Yeah, but it's needed", I said.

"Oh yeah you're right," he said, "I just wonder what Grace and Pearman would say if they were here today."

"Pearman?" his words threw me off so I had to inquire further, "who's that?"

He proceeded to give me insight, "Pearman is the guy who the North Bound Bridge is named for."

I couldn't believe that I had been across and learned so much about the bridge but didn't know that. I asked the guy his name as I prepared to rush home, "Lieutenant Harris," he said.

As I drove home I thought about how much people can impact your life in just a short period of time; this guy had sparked something in me to write my speech for the meeting.

When I got home I looked up the history of the Cooper River Bridge and although the Grace Bridge had been built and opened in 1929, the Pearman Bridge, which was parallel to it, didn't open until 1966. I also learned the Grace Bridge had undergone construction several times to improve it. That night, I stayed up until 2 a.m. reading about that bridge and jotting down notes for my speech. Two weeks later I was sitting in a ballroom along with the rest of the company leaders and it was almost time for my 20 minute keynote address. When Franklin stood to introduce me and recounted how we met at the hotel, my stomach began to rumble; I was so nervous about presenting to this group. I opened my portfolio to glance at my notes and thought I was going to pass out. There was not a single note written on any page in the portfolio. I remembered saying to myself that I wanted to use the new portfolio and I would switch the contents but obviously that never happened and now everyone was clapping because Franklin was finished; it was time for me to go up. I stood and walked toward the podium. I couldn't even remember what the title of my speech was. As I arrived and stood behind the microphone, hoping that everyone would just keep eating and not pay me much attention, every eye in the building was on me. I took a sip of the water that they'd placed on the podium, took a deep breath and began my speech.

"Good evening fellow team members! I'm so thankful to work for a company like Canvass. To prove it, I decided to leave my notes at home and bring an empty Canvass in my portfolio. Today, I've been asked to present to a group of leaders that I highly respect. So what do I say to those who are responsible for leading the charge for our coveted organization?

Ever since I was a freshman in college I've been building a bridge. This bridge began with a *Firm Foundation*, which represents the time that I spent in college. I then constructed my *Tower*, which represents my career aspirations. Next I built the *Abutment*, which represents my understanding that in order to build and/or lead a great team, you have to learn how to support those who led you first." I saw Rory smile. "I went through a very difficult period in the company and realized that this represents my Suspension Cables, the cables that stretch from the *Tower* to hold up the bridge. Although I never would have volunteered for that experience, I am thankful that I didn't give up because that pressure propelled me to the next level, therefore , today I am able to stand and speak to you from the heart. If you're taking notes, my subject tonight is "*The Road that Everyone Travels.*"

You see, I realized as I prepared for tonight that this past year represents the *Deck* of my bridge. The *Deck* is the roadway portion of a bridge that everyone drives on. As leaders, we have to construct our *Deck* in such a way that others are willing to use it to get to their destination. In 1929, the Grace Bridge that we now know as the Cooper River Bridge, opened in Charleston. It represented the completion of John P. Grace's dream to develop a way to get from Charleston to what we now know as Mount Pleasant. I recently learned that this bridge was just one of the parallel bridges that we now see; the other bridge named for Silas N. Pearman was opened in 1966. Once constructed, it was determined that the Grace Bridge would be for Southbound traffic and the Pearman Bridge would be for Northbound traffic.

Over this past year, I have learned a valuable lesson in leadership. I learned that although you may have a bridge that your team is willing to follow, if you give them a chance, they'll produce creative ideas to make the road even better. This year, my team and I built a *Deck* that I would be proud for the rest of our company to travel on. It's a *Deck* that has wide lanes to encompass a diverse array of vehicles. As I cross the Cooper River Bridge daily headed to the office, I notice that there are all different types of cars. They all have the capacity to travel at different speeds, they all have different options, they all have different colors. When I look at our workforce, we're a lot like these cars and the beauty is they all have the ability to take us from one side to the other.

In closing, as we travel this road together, let's ensure that we realize that our car isn't the only one that can get us from one side to the other. I'd like to challenge each leader to return to your offices and regions and live by the *E.A.G.L.E.* Principle:

1. *Encourage* your team to develop new ideas.
2. *Allow* everyone to dream, regardless of title.
3. *Give* your team the freedom to take risks.
4. *Lead* in such a way that mistakes result in learnings, not lashings
5. *Enthusiastically* celebrate successes along the way.

If you implement this principle with your teams, they won't just fly, they'll soar! Thank you."

After I finished, they graciously gave me a standing ovation. I couldn't believe that I had completed the entire speech without any notes. I was thankful for all of the people who had helped me gain insight along the way. When Rodney stood up to close out, there was an announcement I hadn't expected; I was named Manager of the Year. Needless to say, I couldn't wait to return to celebrate with my team.

Points to Ponder

- Don't overlook the gifts inside of those you've been chosen to lead.
- Don't be afraid to take risks in order to break new ground.

- ***E.A.G.L.E.***
    1. *Encourage* your team to develop new ideas.
    2. *Allow* everyone to dream, regardless of title.
    3. *Give* your team the freedom to take risks.
    4. *Lead* in such a way that mistakes result in learnings not lashings.
    5. *Enthusiastically* celebrate successes along the way.

"...although you may have a bridge that your team is willing to follow, if you give them a chance, they'll produce creative ideas to make the road even better."

7

INSPIRING OTHERS TO BUILD THEIR BRIDGE

IT'S ANOTHER YEAR of celebration as I prepare to attend my 10-year college class reunion and things at Canvass are great as the Charleston office continues to grow. Our innovative ideas have spread company-wide and we are all experiencing the benefits. I got married three years ago; we have a little one and expecting another.

The new bridge has opened and is now called the Ravenal Bridge. It's much bigger and a lot more beautiful than the old bridges but I must admit that I miss them. I'll miss them even more in a few months when I move back to Greenville. Canvass has now created a new position for me they are calling the V.P.D.D. which stands for Vice President of Developing Dreams. I requested that I assume my new role in Greenville where the company doesn't presently have an office. As I prepare for the move, I'm thankful to be returning home but I will leave a lot of great memories here in the *"lowcountry"*.

Yesterday I received a call from Professor Humbert asking if I'd do him a favor. I'm not sure why he asks for favors when he never accepts no for an answer. He asked if I would speak to a group of potential students and parents during one of the major open house weekends for CofC; it happened to be the same weekend as our class reunion so things worked out perfectly. I had conquered all of my fears of Public Speaking but had now grown accustomed to talking about our business; I was very excited to accept the invitation but really didn't know what to say. I didn't want to bore a group of potential students with info about Canvass and be the reason that they choose a different school. I asked my wife what she thought I should speak about and she began to rattle off some mind numbing statistics that still have my brain aching. I thanked her for her suggestions and then took an aspirin and went to sleep.

On Saturday of that week, my son and I took a walk on the Ravenal Bridge. As we crossed over, I heard a little boy ask his dad how they built the big bridge. "I don't know son", he said and before I knew it, I was dumping all the knowledge I had learned about the bridges right at their feet. After the guy thanked me and walked away swiftly, I knew what I would speak to the group about. I had become a *Bridge Builder* and didn't even realize it. As a *Bridge Builder*, it was my responsibility to help others get from one side to the other and though I could share all of my life experiences with them and allow them to cross my bridge, I realized what I gained through my experience of having to build my own was invaluable.

I am so thankful for the people like Professor Humbert, Rory and Pastor Dogan who inspired me along the way. People like Franklin, Owen and George Benson who believed in me and gave me a chance. I'm even thankful for Edward Boyles who confirmed how strong I am by placing me under immense pressure. There are so many people prior to these folks like my mom and my aunts who instilled great values in me along with friends and co-workers who gave me a piece of them along the way; I remember them all. The truth is that my bridge was built by a large construction crew, some of which stayed in my life from start to finish like the primary contractors on a bridge project and others who came in for a season to do their part like a subcontractor but I am thankful to each of them for their amazing contribution to my life.

It's class reunion weekend and it's so good to see everyone. Some of the group has found out about my speech, thanks to Professor Humbert, and will now be sitting in the balcony to attend. Friday night was a blur as we all tried to relive every college story and sentimental location possible. Needless to say, 8 a.m. came early after we laid down at 4 a.m. It's 9 a.m. and I'm in the auditorium having a cup of coffee and enjoying the bagels that they brought in for the Continental Breakfast. I'm speaker number seven so I have a little time to wake up and get my juices flowing. I called in a favor to a local construction company who was a client of ours and they donated some materials and since my friends were adamant about attending, I gave them a job to do.

When I stood to speak, each student received a hard hat that said *"Building Bridges"* on the front. I then placed one on my head that said, *"The Bridge Builder"*. I told them that the hat represented an occupation that we all have been employed to do for a portion of our lives, we just might not know it yet. I walked them through the process of how I discovered it and told them that today was about giving them a head start; I wanted to share all of the principles I'd learned like *M.O.V.E., T.O.W.E.R., S.T.A.N.D., F.I.G.H.T.* and *E.A.G.L.E.* but realized that those principles were best embraced at specific stages of their bridge so I was just going to give them an overarching principle for the entire journey instead: *B.R.I.D.G.E.*

1. *Believe* that you can make it to the other side.
2. *Rely* on the wisdom of those around you who have taken similar journeys.
3. *Invest* in peer relationships that will encourage you to stay focused.
4. *Define* the path that you plan to take.
5. *Gain* strength from the most difficult times.
6. *Expand* your bridge as needed.

When I was done, everyone gave me a standing ovation and I shook Professor Humbert's hand as he was coming to introduce the next speaker; it felt like I was graduating all over again. "Let's give another hand for WARREN IVERSON NICHOLS," he said. At that moment, I realized this was my destiny; I was born to *W.I.N.*

ABOUT THE AUTHOR

Zachary Brewster, PHR, is Chief Visionary Officer at The Bridge Builder (www.thebridgebuilder.net). For over a decade he has aided organizations in talent acquisition, workforce development and strategic planning. He has had the privilege of working with Fortune 100-Fortune 500 Companies, Colleges and Universities, Civic and Community Organizations.

www.ingramcontent.com/pod-product-compliance
Lightning Source LLC
Chambersburg PA
CBHW070846180526
45168CB00002B/976